Mother Earth Needs Our Help!

By Esther Sampedro
Illustrated by Sarah Vazquez

This book is dedicated to my daughter, Ashley and my son, Ian and to all of the children of the world to whom we grownups owe a vibrant, beautiful and healthy planet.

Let us all protect the world we live in!

Order this book online at www.trafford.com
or email orders@trafford.com

Most Trafford titles are also available at major online book retailers.

Illustrated by Sarah Vazquez

Printed in the United States of America.

ISBN: 978-1-4269-3083-6

Library of Congress Control Number: 2010904382

Trafford rev. 11/02/2011

Trafford
PUBLISHING® www.trafford.com

North America & international
toll-free: 1 888 232 4444 (USA & Canada)
phone: 250 383 6864 ♦ fax: 812 355 4082

PROLOGUE

People love what they can understand, and they take care of what they love. The process of teaching you and all kids like you to love Earth and everything that's inside it, starts by making you understand how our planet works. A kid who understands why that "small cover" that surrounds and protects earth is so important is a child who could eventually become an atmospheric scientist, for example. It will also be a kid who is motivated to help maintain that atmosphere clean. What are you waiting for? Mother earth needs you to understand how to take care of her!

Angela Posada-Swafford,
Science and Exploration Writer

"Mother Earth needs our help!" says the Sun.

"What is wrong with her?" asks the Moon.

"Her blankie has a boo boo," says the Sun.

"A boo boo?" asks the Moon.

"She has discovered her blankie has a small hole. She is afraid it is coming undone and it will not protect her anymore," says the Sun.

"How serious is that?" asks the Moon.

"It is very serious," says the Sun.

"Her blankie protects Mother Earth from the cold and hot weather. It keeps her feeling good all the time! But mostly, Mother Earth is worried because her blankie is getting dirty," says the Sun.

"What do you mean dirty?" asks the Moon.

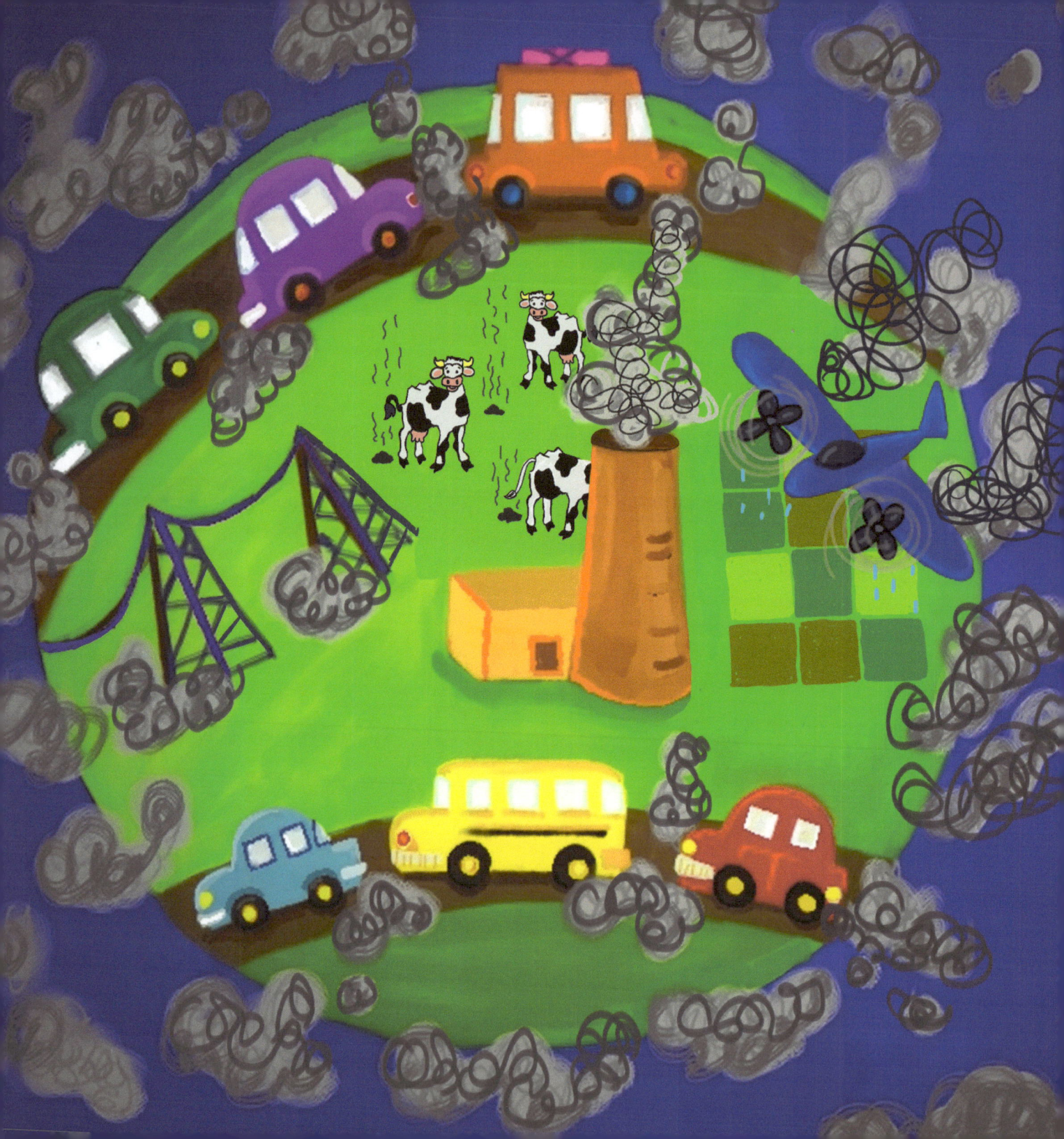

"Cars, farms, factories and electrical power plants produce clouds of smoke, which makes her cough. These clouds are not going away and they are trapping the heat from my rays making Mother Earth feel very hot."

"The heat causes the water to evaporate. As a result, the rivers and the lakes are beginning to dry out," says the Sun.

"What about the ocean?" asks the Moon.

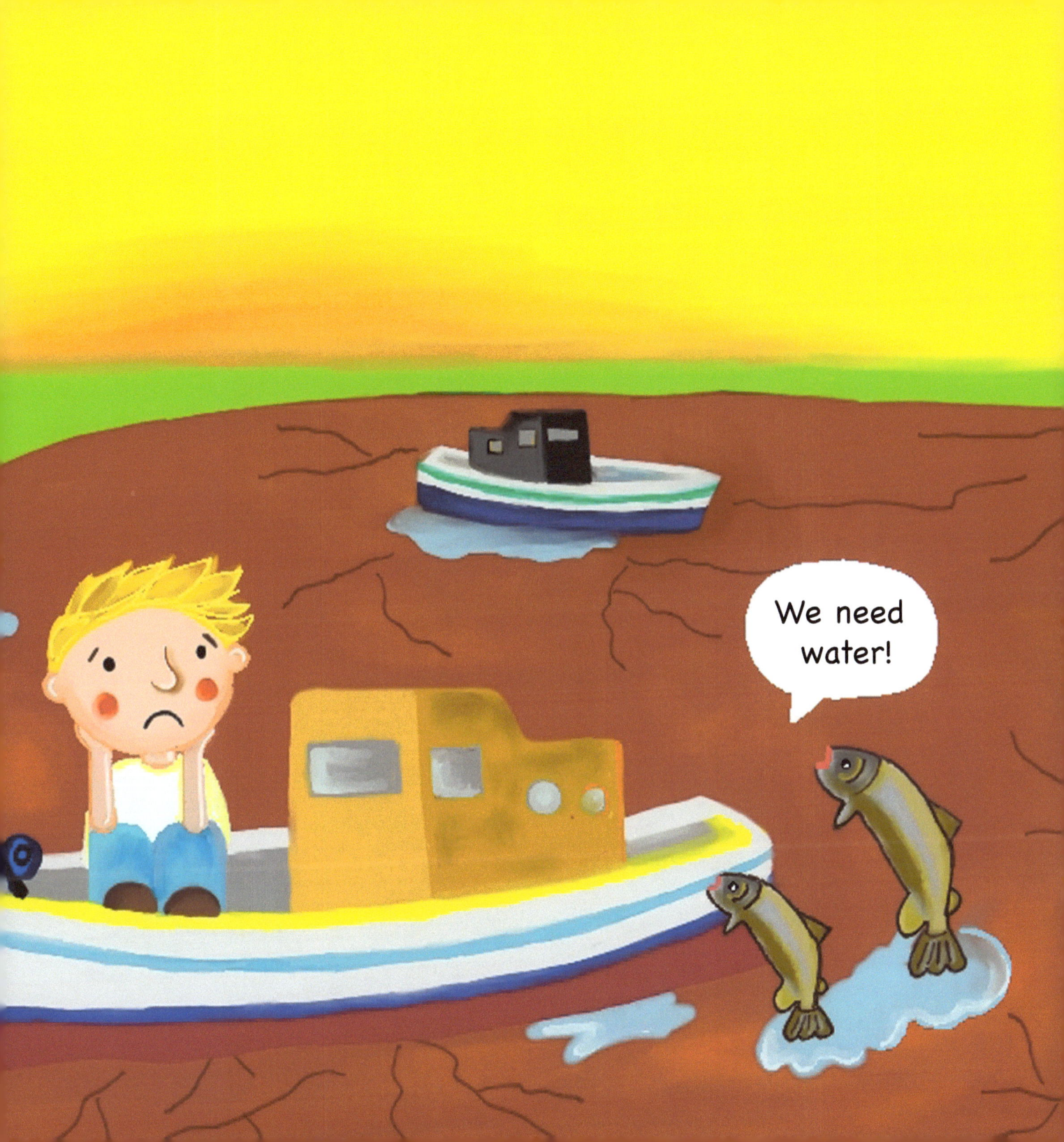

"Well, the water of the ocean is also getting warmer. It is so warm, that the mountains of ice, called glaciers and the ice sheets covering the Arctic Pole, Greenland and Antarctica, are slowly melting away.

"Where is all that fresh water going?" asks the Moon.

"Back to the ocean, causing the sea to rise," says the Sun.

"Oh no! That is not safe for the people, animals and plants that live on islands and coastal cities all around the world," says the Moon.

"The melting of the ice is preventing Mother Earth from balancing her body temperature and feeling good," says the Sun.

"What can people do to help Mother Earth feel good?" asks the Moon.

"People must stop polluting her sky with smoke, her land with poisonous chemicals and her ocean and rivers with trash," says the Sun.

"How does pollution makes her feel?" asks the Moon.

"Pollution makes her feel icky! It causes her nose to itch making her sneeze!" says the Sun.

"What happens when she sneezes?" asks the Moon.

"Sometimes in the form of a hurricane, she makes loud noises before she blows away everything on her path. Other times she spins in a tornado."

"There are times she cries and cries flooding everything on her way. Sometimes her tears get frozen making lots of snow and ice, stranding people in their homes, cars, schools and buildings"

"When she stops crying, she feels dry and itchy and erupts in wildfires," says the Sun.

"I got it!" says the Moon. "Now, I understand why Mother Earth is feeling so sad, pollution is the number one reason."

"Absolutely right!" exclaims the Sun.

"Garbage is everywhere, in the rivers and lakes, in the mountains and meadows, in the ocean. This is unhealthy for children. And, animals mistakenly eat plastic and foam for food, getting ill."

"Men are cutting the trees of her beautiful forests sometimes to build homes, make furniture and produce paper," says the Sun.

"This can not be good," cries the Moon. "The trees produce oxygen and they help clean Mother Earth's air!"

EXTINCT ANIMALS

Cosmos
Astrosanguineus

Keulemans
Laughing Owl

Dodo

Dusky Seaside
Sparrow

Tasmanian Wolf

Panthera Tigris

Deloneura
Immaculata

Spanish Ibex

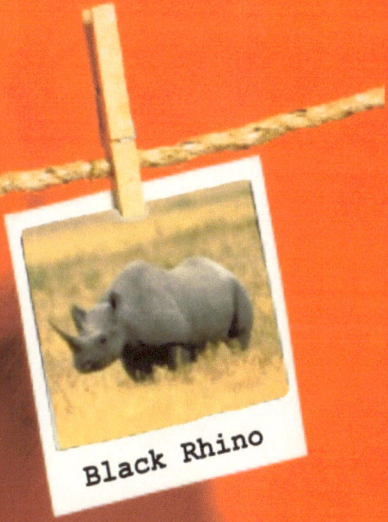
Black Rhino

Golden Toad

"These are the reasons why her friends the animals and the plants are getting sick and some are dying," sadly replies the Sun.

"She wants to help them but, she cannot do it alone. She needs children to help." says the Sun.

"What can children do to help her?" asks the Moon.

"They must stop throwing garbage on the street," says the Sun. "Pick it up, collect it and put it in the trashcan. When possible they can reduce, reuse and recycle anything in their daily life. Mother Earth will be very happy!"

"They need to save paper. Saving paper saves trees. They need to save water. Make it quick and make it fun!"

"When they leave their room, bathroom or any other room in their house they must turn the lights off. This saves energy!

They need to turn off the TV, the computer and the radio if they are not using them. These electronic devices produce a lot of heat and use a lot of electricity!" says the Sun.

"On breezy days they can open their windows and turn off the air conditioning," says the Sun.

"Perhaps, this will be a good time to go out and fly a kite," says the Moon.

"They can show Mom and Dad how much fun it is to ride a bike, to walk in a nearby park, to plant a tree, to play games and activities in the backyard, to spend a night out with the stars," says the Sun.

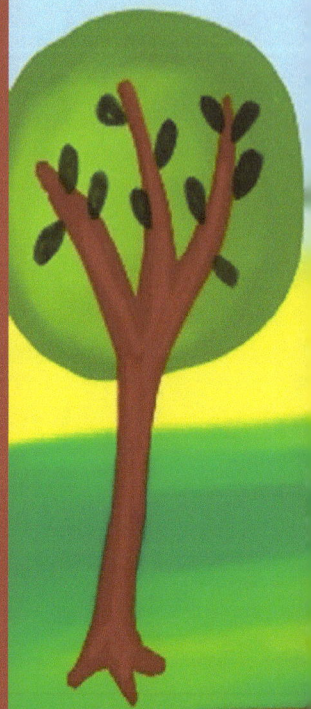

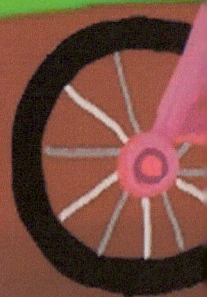

"And, to play, *bug detective!*" says the Moon. "The garden is filled with lots of crawling creatures!"

"They can buy less, reuse more, share as much with siblings, neighbors and friends, and live simply. They can tell their mommy and daddy, brother and sister and their friends how to help Mother Earth," affirms the Sun.

"And, they must love Mother Earth like they love their mommy! There is no one like her!" exclaims the Moon.

"Perhaps we can help too," says the Sun.

"How?" asks the Moon.

"I will touch Mother Earth only with my good solar rays," says the Sun.

"And every night," says the Moon, "I will shine like a star, providing plenty of light, as a safe pathway for children and their parents to enjoy an evening walk."

"She is fragile, she is special, and she is unique!" says the Sun.

"She is a great role model for us all, she nourishes without discriminating," says the Moon.

"Let us all take care of Mother Earth!" announces the Sun.

"The smallest of changes make a world of difference"

—*Esther Sampedro, Founder of Kids Love Mother Earth*—

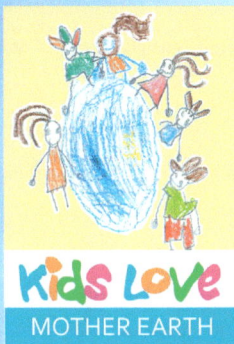

A child is the essence of love. Teaching children to love themselves from within is the first step in inspiring in them respect, compassion, and empathy for "Mother Earth." The mission of **Kids Love Mother Earth** is to teach children through the language of love the unique relationship and fragile balance between humans, animals and plants and our planet the Earth.

Kids Love Mother Earth is a 501 c3 non-profit organization founded in 2008 by Esther Sampedro. KLME is based in Miami, Florida. All of the proceeds for this book are donated to KLME.

Learn more about **Kids Love Mother Earth** on the official Web site:

www.klme.org

www.ingramcontent.com/pod-product-compliance
Lightning Source LLC
Chambersburg PA
CBHW042011080426

42734CB00002B/42